"Never Empty the Spit Valve on Yourself."

And Other Life Lessons Learned in Middle School Band

Compiled and Illustrated by

Dr. Emery Warnock

WestBow
PRESS
A DIVISION OF THOMAS NELSON

WestBow books may be ordered through booksellers or by contacting:

WestBow Press
A Division of Thomas Nelson
1663 Liberty Drive
Bloomington, IN 47403
www.westbowpress.com
1-(866) 928-1240

Because of the dynamic nature of the Internet, any web addresses or links contained in this book may have changed since publication and may no longer be valid. The views expressed in this work are solely those of the author and do not necessarily reflect the views of the publisher, and the publisher hereby disclaims any responsibility for them.

Any people depicted in stock imagery provided by Thinkstock are models, and such images are being used for illustrative purposes only.

Certain stock imagery © Thinkstock.

ISBN: 978-1-4497-6118-9 (e)
ISBN: 978-1-4497-6119-6 (sc)

Library of Congress Control Number: 2012913670

Printed in the United States of America

WestBow Press rev. date: 07/31/2012

Foreword

In 2010, I became a middle school band director's wife. Up to this point, I had taken a few piano lessons, but never participated in a school music ensemble. While I loved music, school music to me seemed a nice extracurricular activity that was peripheral to the core academic subjects. As I met my husband's students, their parents and grandparents (as well as countless friends, colleagues and clients in my own research career), I soon learned the vital, life-changing role of school music. Conversations began to sound like a broken record to me: "So what does your husband-to-be do? Oh, band director. I was in band and loved it. It was such hard work, but so rewarding. It changed my life." What really impressed me was the wide variety of career paths in which these former band students had excelled. Very few, if any, had played music professionally. Most did not even play music in college, but the lessons learned had truly shaped their lives and character in indelible ways that they often credited with their later success.

While at an end-of-the-year band picnic, several of the parents and grandparents again began to spontaneously tell me about the impact of band on their student's life. For one family, the band student looked forward to school every day and was significantly more driven and ambitious than any other child in the family. For another, band had given the child a place to belong during the awkward middle school years. For yet another who struggled with emotional issues, band had become an outlet for expression.

There is no question that school music complements academic subjects and instills key character values almost effortlessly. In practicing a difficult piece and overcoming the challenge, students learn their own potential and reward of hard work. In learning to allow a solo to stand out in the ensemble, students learn to play a supporting role for the success of the whole. The profound place of school music is recognized even by current students that are not yet teenagers. After hearing so many stories, I encouraged my husband to compile some of the bits of wisdom from his students to help him get through the days when it feels you have no purpose. It is our hope that the reader, too, will enjoy and gain inspiration from these quotes.

Susanna Warnock
Senoia, GA

Life Lessons on
Music

"Music can change how you feel."

—6th Grade, Alto Saxophone

"The most fun songs come from the most simple rhythms."

—8th Grade, Clarinet

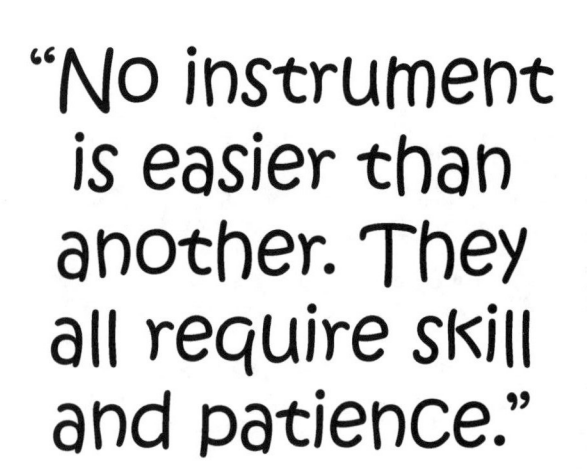

"No instrument
is easier than
another. They
all require skill
and patience."

—8th Grade, Trombone

"Music is empowering."

—7th Grade, Clarinet

"An instrument is an extension of your voice."

—8th Grade, Trumpet

"My trumpet has changed who I am."

—7th Grade, Trumpet

"Playing loud
is not the
purpose."

—6th Grade, Alto Saxophone

"Count your rests whenever you have rests because if you don't play in time, it can become a mess."

—7th Grade, Oboe

"Music is a
gift to anyone
who wishes
to play it."

—8th Grade, Euphonium

"Don't empty the spit valve on yourself."

—7th Grade, Tuba

"Not everything in life is important. Music is important."

—8th Grade, Euphonium

Life Lessons on
Facing
Problems

"Life has crescendos and decrescendos, but it will end out fine."

—8th Grade, Trumpet

"I learned humility from messing up and dealing with it."

—8th Grade, Percussion

"Be patient with yourself, and take the time to learn."

—6th Grade, Percussion

"If anything is hard, slow it down a little."

—7th Grade, Clarinet

"Keep your chin up—literally."

—7th Grade, Alto Saxophone

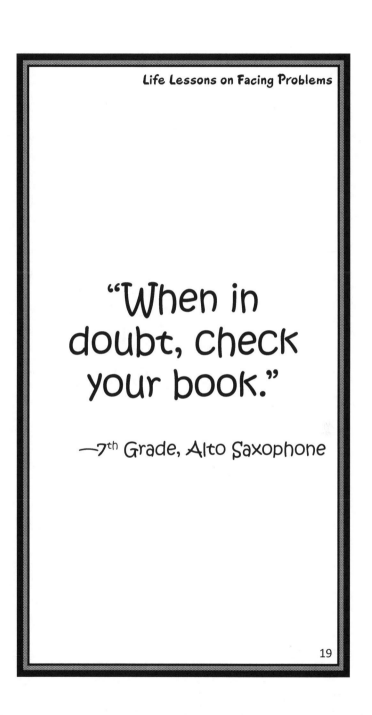

"When in doubt, check your book."

—7th Grade, Alto Saxophone

"Most things only look difficult."

—7th Grade, Alto Saxophone

Life Lessons on
Being
Yourself

"Band makes
me feel good
at something."

—6th Grade, Flute

"Sometimes you have to focus on you, if everyone's part is different."

—7th Grade, Clarinet

"Be true to yourself. I'm a band kid. I'm proud. People aren't weird because they're in band."

—6th Grade, Clarinet

"Believe in yourself. If you're too hard on yourself, you'll always be afraid to improve."

—8th Grade, Trumpet

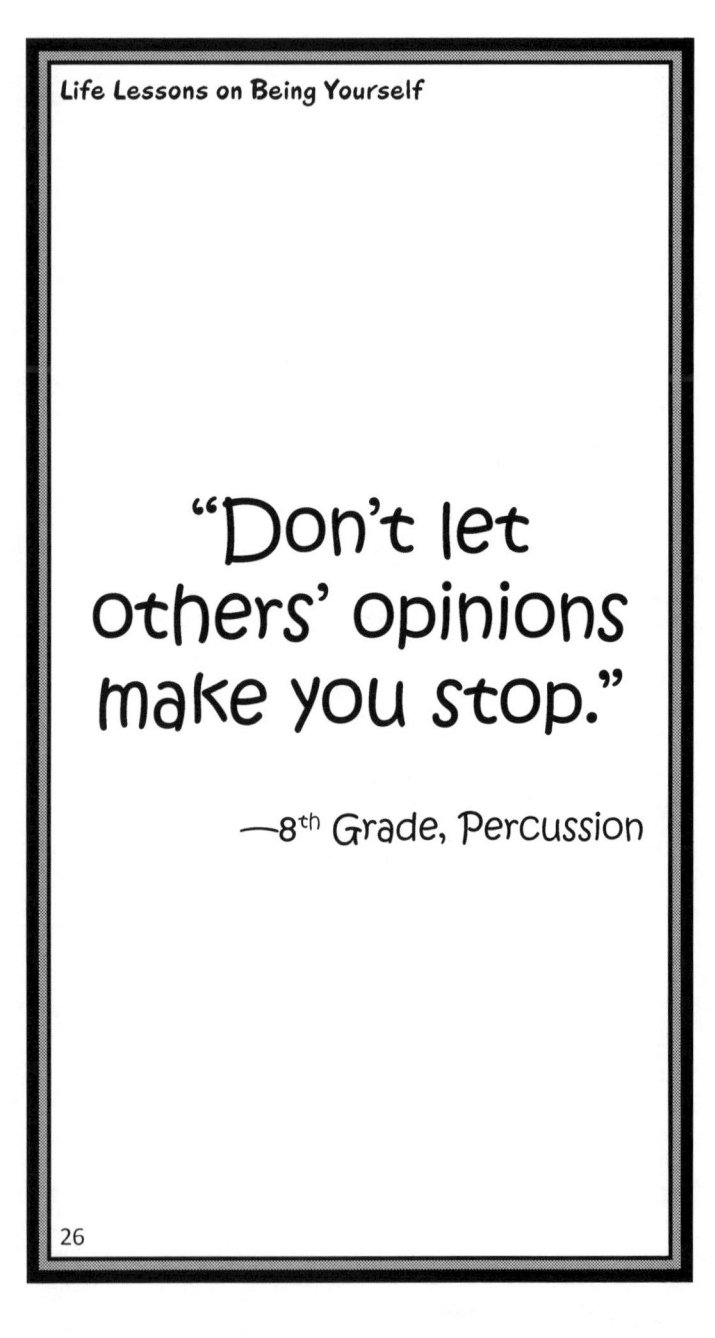

"Don't let others' opinions make you stop."

—8th Grade, Percussion

"Everyone
is a work in
progress; no
one is perfect."

—7th Grade, Trumpet

"Even if you have a little part, it means a lot."

—6th Grade, Alto Saxophone

"Band is like a wonderful homing beacon that helped me discover what I really am capable of doing here."

—8th Grade, Trumpet

—7th Grade, Percussion

"I feel like myself in band."

"Do what you love and don't listen to people if they make fun of you."

—8th Grade, Flute

Life Lessons on
Working Together

"Even if the flutes speed up, the saxophones might be out of tune. I shouldn't berate the flutes."

—8th Grade, Alto Saxophone

"It's good to be a part of something more than just yourself."

—8th Grade, Contra Alto Clarinet

"Stick together no matter how hard things are."

—7th Grade, Clarinet

"Life isn't about you. There's always someone better."

—8th Grade, Percussion

"Teams only work if I pull my own weight."

—8th Grade, Alto Saxophone

"Band can bring
you to friends
that care
about you no
matter what."

—6th Grade, Trombone

"If someone is having trouble, help them out, and you'll get something out of it, too."

—8th Grade, Trumpet

"Always listen to others' ideas. It could help improve yourself."

—7th Grade, Bassoon

"Don't
overpower
other people
just because
you can."

—8th Grade, Trombone

"Band is like my family. We watch out for each other and support one another. We're a dysfunctional family sometimes, but a family nonetheless."

—8th Grade, Trumpet

Life Lessons on
Having
a Good
Attitude

"Keep life on a steady beat."

—8th Grade, Trumpet

"Do your best, have fun, and be serious all at the same time."

—6th Grade, French Horn

"Playing trumpet can relieve stress."

—7th Grade, Trumpet

"Beauty is everywhere. Even the most irritating piece can be beautiful with effort."

—7th Grade, Alto Saxophone

"Always be ready to learn new stuff. You never know what will come next."

—8th Grade, Trombone

"Don't judge a person by what they look like, because they may be amazing at playing."

—6th Grade, Clarinet

"Be nice to people who are still learning. Learning takes time, and some people won't be as talented as you."

—6th Grade, Percussion

"Get comfortable with unknown things."

—7th Grade, Clarinet

"Try new things. I had never played an instrument before in my life."

—6th Grade, Clarinet

"If we are mad, the music sounds mad. If we are sad, the music sounds sad. If we are happy, the music sounds happy."

—8th Grade, Trumpet

Life Lessons on
Discipline

"Don't dream
things if you
are not going to
work for them."

—8th Grade, Clarinet

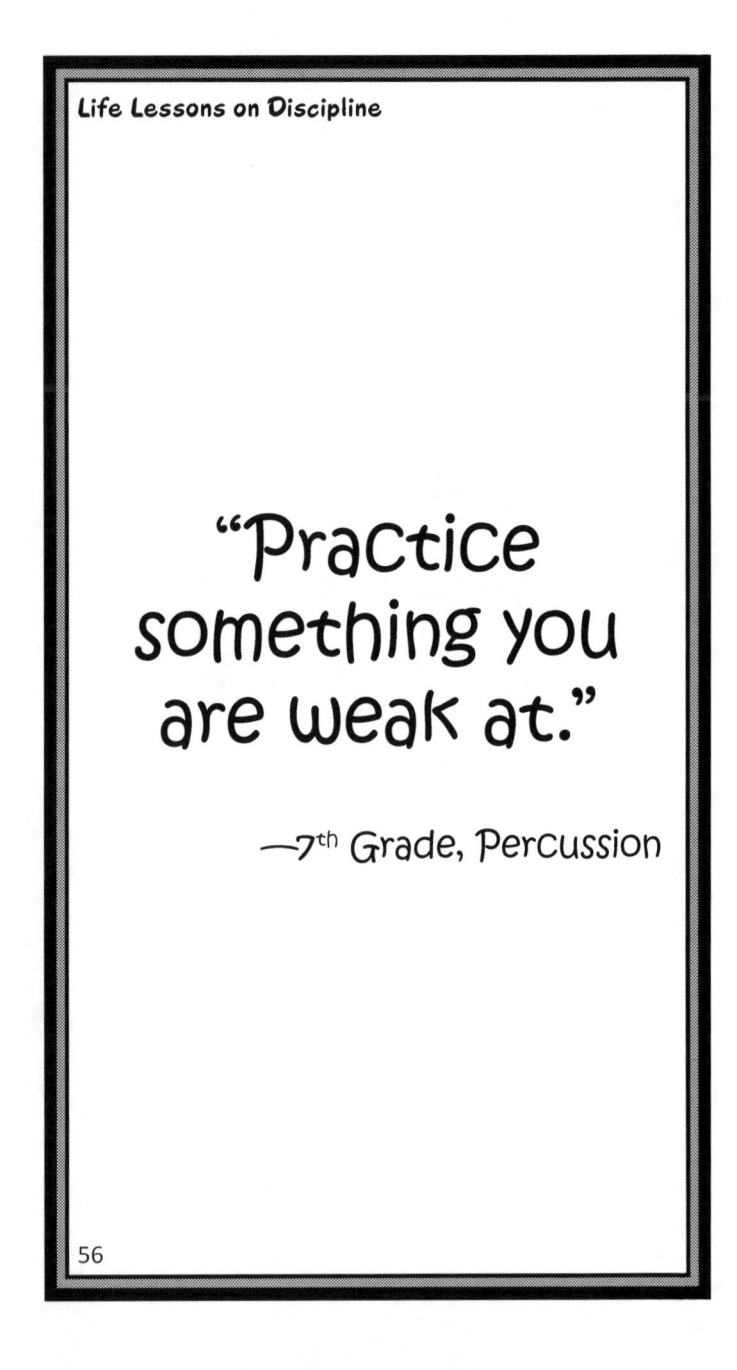

"Practice something you are weak at."

—7th Grade, Percussion

"Listen before doing."

—8th Grade, Trombone

"I learned to control myself when others are being stupid."

—6th Grade, Percussion

"Don't act like you can do something when you can't."

—7th Grade, Flute

"Behave and you will have more opportunities."

—6th Grade, Percussion

"Don't talk when other people are playing because it turns out to be a loud mess."

—7th Grade, Oboe

"Ignore annoying people—other students, not <u>teachers!</u>"

—6th Grade, Percussion

"Be quiet when you're bored."

—6th Grade, Percussion

Success
Life Lessons on

"To succeed,
be passionate
about what
you're doing."

—8th Grade, Trombone

"Don't waste your time. Do whatever you can to be at the top."

—6th Grade, Flute

"No matter where you are, always do your best."

—7th Grade, Tenor Saxophone

"Self-satisfaction is the best prize."

—7th Grade, Alto Saxophone

"Fixing little things will make the entire band sound better."

—7th Grade, Trumpet

"Having fun
can help you
succeed."

—6th Grade, Trombone

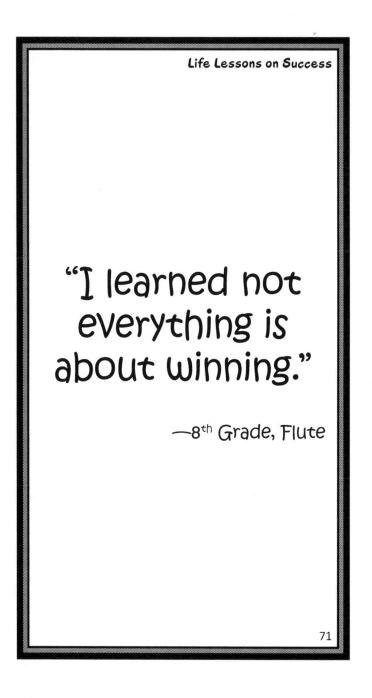

"I learned not everything is about winning."

—8th Grade, Flute

"Be slow to
speak and
quick to listen
and you'll do
just fine."

—8th Grade, Percussion

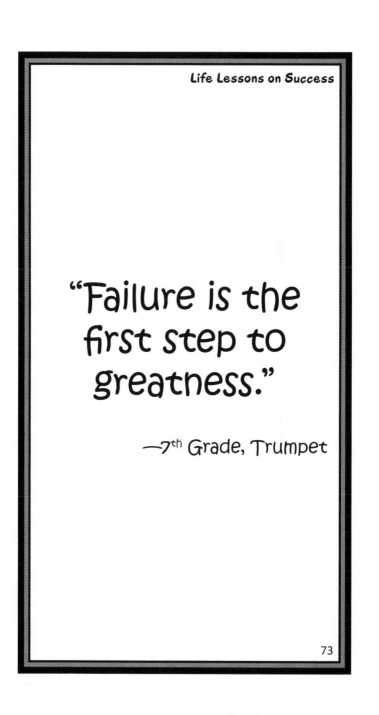

"Failure is the first step to greatness."

—7th Grade, Trumpet

"As soon as you think you know everything, a million new ideas will pop up to learn."

—8th Grade, Trombone

Life Lessons on
Daily Living

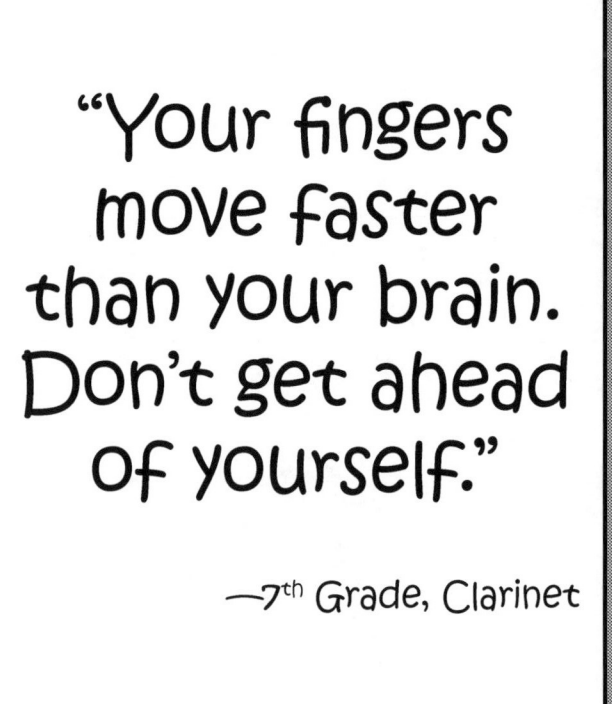

"Your fingers move faster than your brain. Don't get ahead of yourself."

—7th Grade, Clarinet

"Put your heart into what you love."

—6th Grade, Percussion

"Band is a good way to get my family together."

—7th Grade, Clarinet

"The faster you go, the harder it will be."

—8th Grade, Trumpet

"You can have a fun time up to a point to where you need to stop."

—8th Grade, Trumpet

"Teachers will laugh at the funniest jokes."

—7th Grade, Alto Saxophone

"Clarinets are amazing kissers."

—7th Grade, Alto Saxophone

"Take care of the things you care about."

—6th Grade, Trombone

"Endurance is key; patience is a necessity; cooperating is best; and never give up."

—8th Grade, Percussion

"Whatever the question, air is the answer (most of the time)."

—8th Grade, Clarinet

"Keep mean stuff in your head or whisper it to the person next to you."

—8th Grade, Trumpet

"If you don't want to get hiccups, breathe right."

—7th Grade, Clarinet

"Band and
gum don't go
together."

—7th Grade, Alto Saxophone